THE SECRET GARDEN

100 FLORAL RADIOGRAPHS

by

ALBERT G. RICHARDS

Albert G Richards

1998

First Edition

**Library of Congress Cataloging in
Publication Data**

The Secret Garden

90-83101

PUBLISHER: ALMAR COMPANY
P.O. BOX 15174
ANN ARBOR, MICHIGAN 48104
ISBN 0-9628791-0-X

Contents

100 Floral Radiographs arranged alphabetically

About the Author

Dedication

This book is dedicated to my wife, Marian, for her loving help and encouragement in the preparation of this book, which gives us a glimpse into the secret garden of flowers.

Acknowledgements

Listed in alphabetical order are my friends who, each in their own unique way, unselfishly contributed to make this book possible.

Larry Angelosante
Clarence Dukes
Annie Hannan
Guenter Schmitt
Kathleen Richards
Barbara Rosens
Samuel Ursu

INTRODUCTION

Ever since Wilhelm Roentgen discovered the X ray in 1895, scientists have passed X rays through everything from shells and bugs to plants and people. X-ray pictures, called radiographs, are similar to photographs in that they record the outline or silhouette of a subject. But where a photograph records the surface details, a radiograph registers a subject's interior structures.

Albert G. Richards, an Emeritus Professor of Dentistry from the University of Michigan School of Dentistry, does not claim to be the first person to x-ray flowers. His success with the process as it relates to flowers, however, has yielded the most spectacular results.

One afternoon in 1960, Richards made a modest purchase that marked a turning point in his life. He bought a bunch of daffodils for twenty-seven cents, took them back to the dental school, and made his first floral radiograph. It wasn't very good, but it piqued his interest and formed the cornerstone of a new avocation for him. Now, 3,000 radiographs later, his collection of floral radiographs includes blossoms from trees, vines, bulbs and both annual and perennial herbaceous plants.

In the photographic tradition of Edward Weston, Imogene Cunningham, and more recently, Irving Penn and Robert Mapplethorpe, Albert Richards achieves a directness and oriental austerity in his works by altering the familiar designs of nature. Unique to the X-ray process is the ability to reveal shape, form, and texture — all within a single exposure.

Barbara Rosens

Barbara Rosens

THE SECRET GARDEN

*"Of course, there will always be those who look only
at technique who ask 'how,' while others of more
curious nature will ask 'why.' Personally, I have always
preferred inspiration to information."* — Man Ray

*A beautiful blossom is a fleeting thing,
It stays for a moment and then takes wing;
With special rays we catch it ere flight
So all may enjoy the beautiful sight.*

While many people love and appreciate flowers, they may never realize or see the secret beauty that is hidden within the blossoms. One way we perceive beauty is with our eyes. When we close our eyes, we cannot see the beautiful flowers around us. Even with our eyes open, we see only that portion of the flower that is nearest to us. In a rose, the nearest petals hide from our view all of its secret details that lie beyond; so much of the beauty of the blossom is hidden. With the penetrating power of the X ray, floral radiographs reveal the details in all the successive layers of petals and other tissues.

Radiography, whether it is industrial, medical, dental, or floral, is basically a photographic process whereby an object is exposed to X rays, and its image is cast upon a sheet of X-ray film. In photography, the film is located within a camera equipped with a lens. A tiny image is cast on the film by the visible rays of light which enter the camera after reflecting from the surface of an object. After the film has been processed, the images can then be enlarged and printed on photographic paper. There is no camera or lens involved in the radiographic process. When a radiograph is made of an ailing tooth, for example, the X-ray machine is positioned near the patient's face and a film packet is inserted on the other side of the tooth, next to the tongue. The image of the tooth is always slightly larger than life-size, and the internal anatomy of the tooth is displayed within its silhouette. These same factors apply when making a floral radiograph (an X-ray picture of a flower).

The science of radiography is based on the fact that X rays can penetrate through an object, whereas visible light cannot. Therefore, X rays enable one to "see" within the object. As the rays pass through the object, they are attenuated differently by portions of the object that are either thicker, denser or composed of higher atomic number elements, than are other parts.

When x-raying iron castings, broken bones, teeth or flowers, the penetrating power of the X ray must be adjusted to optimize the way the differences in thickness and composition of the object record on the film. The images are always in shades of black and white, since the phenomenon of color does not exist in the X-ray spectrum. The process does not require the introduction of any chemicals into the flower nor is the flower harmed by its small exposure to X rays. The type of shadows produced by side-lighting in photography does not occur in floral radiography.

As with normal photography, movement by the specimen will cause a blurred image. In floral radiography, several factors may cause movement. It may be caused by the change in temperature from the hot outdoors, where the flower grew, to the cooler temperature of the X-ray laboratory. Some flowers, when harvested, must be placed in water immediately, or they will wilt. Others are sturdier and survive in air without wilting for a longer time. When cutting an Oriental Poppy flower, it is necessary to have a cigarette lighter on hand so the end of the stem can be seared quickly before it is placed in water. Following this treatment, the Poppy will maintain its form for a day or more. When an open Tulip is brought in from the bright sunlit garden to the more dimly lit X-ray laboratory, it begins to close up, perhaps sensing the approach of nighttime. Some flowers, like the Cosmos, seem to follow the sun, so harvesting the flower should be delayed until the blossom forms a pleasing composition with the stem and leaves.

Great care is exercised in choosing and preparing a flower that is to be recorded. The chosen blossom should be fresh and undamaged. Clean flowers, in prime condition, are the starting point for making beautiful floral radiographs. Foreign materials, hidden within a blossom, would be visible on a radiograph, and therefore must be eliminated before radiographing the flower. Occasionally, a hidden insect is discovered that also must be removed. Dewdrops and raindrops record as ugly spots on the flower's image. These drops of moisture can be removed either by waiting for them to evaporate naturally or by absorbing them with pointed strips of blotting paper carefully inserted between the petals.

Wind and rain may deposit solid particles of dirt on a blossom. Some particles can be removed by the careful use of a tiny brush. Other particles, lodged deeply within a flower, can be removed with a miniature vacuum cleaner with probes shaped like large hypodermic needles. Debris adhering to the petals and fuzzy stems of some flowers can be carefully removed with sticky cellophane tape. Flowers grown in a greenhouse are usually much cleaner than those grown outdoors.

The difference between what one sees directly or records photographically and what is displayed in a floral radiograph is nicely illustrated by the Calla Lily (Fig. 14) and the Jack-in-the-Pulpit (Fig. 55). Only the tip of the spadex in the center of the blossom was visible to the eye or would record on a photograph, whereas the entire spadex is displayed in the radiograph. Also the ability to see details through the successive layers which surround the spadex certainly adds to the allure of the beautiful lines and form of these blossoms.

We use flowers to speak for us. On happy occasions we send flowers to express our joy, and on sad occasions to convey our sorrow. It seems that flowers also speak to each other (Fig. 55). It appears that the Jack-in-the-Pulpit on the left got his nose punched in for interrupting while the larger flower on the right was speaking.

A beautiful Cup and Saucer Campanula is shown in Figure 15. That portion of the saucer which lies beyond the cup shows on the radiograph by would not have been seen by an observer nor would it have appeared on a photograph. This particular blossom was purple, others were pink and white. X-ray pictures do not distinguish between colors; only shape or variations in the thickness and composition of the tissues are recorded. Looking at the lower edge of the saucer and to the right of the stem, one sees the image of a drop of water. This floral radiograph displays minute details such as the tiny hairlike structures on portions of the saucer, stem and leaves.

The small, insignificant-looking blossom of the Chinese Lantern gives rise to a lovely, large orange seed pod in the autumn (Fig. 19). Radiographs of these pods reveal both the elaborate system of veins in the walls of the pods and the seed cluster within.

At the end of each of the five spur-like tubules of the Columbine is a small round organ that secrets nectar. Figure 25 and 26 illustrate how far each tubule has been filled with the nectar. This feature cannot be seen or photographed, but it is readily displayed radiographically.

In Figure 29, all the petals of the Cyclamen blossoms appear to have been blown back, as though they had been subjected to a strong wind. However, this is the normal form of the blossom. The tiny needle-like stigma, projecting from the center of the upper blossom, is clearly visible. The ability to register details in four or more superimposed petals is well documented in this radiograph.

The Daffodil (Fig. 30) is one of our most beautiful early spring flowers. The pistil and other structures within the Daffodil's trumpet are revealed in this radiograph, along with the husk that initially covered the developing flower bud.

The green leaves and the graceful petals of the white Dogwood blossom are rich in details (Fig. 35). The green leaves are clearly seen through the petals in this radiograph, or are the petals clearly seen through the leaves? Spatial relationships are sometimes ambiguous on a radiograph.

The thick succulent petals of the Lily, so rich in details, make it a favorite flower to radiograph (Fig. 59). The reflexed tips of the petals, the curvature of the pistil and stamens and the rich pattern of details all add to the graceful charm of this blossom. There are many different types of Lilies, but each is beautiful in its own right.

The Gloxinia blossom, with its ruffled edges and unopened bud, forms an interesting composition in the radiograph in Figure 44. This image is so detailed that even the hairlike structures on the stems are discernable.

Radiographs of the Iris, one of nature's most lovely flowers, reveal not only the beauty within the falls and standards, but also in the contents of the bud and ovules in Figure 52.

In a radiograph of a Rose (Fig. 80), the petals resemble sheets of gossamer or transparent black chiffon. The number of petals in a single blossom may exceed sixty in some varieties. Ideally, for floral radiography, the blossom should have between twenty-five and thirty petals and have small leaves.

Tulip blossoms come in a myriad of colors, sizes and shapes, but color does not record on a radiograph. Pictured in Figure 92 is a beautifully shaped blossom with lovey, curved petals displaying fine inner details. This is an exceptional image illustrating the basic difference between what one can see with the unaided eye or record photographically, and what is recorded radiographically.

Fuchsia blossoms hang from a vine and frequently appear in pairs. Their radiographic images (Fig. 42) resemble tiny ballerinas pirouetting.

When deciding which Saucer Magnolia blossoms to radiograph, choose ones growing on twigs that extend vertically (Fig. 62). Magnolia buds and blossoms are usually positioned vertically while the lower branches of the tree extend horizontally, thus making a 90 degree angle with the blossom. Radiographs of these blossoms have the stem exiting the side of the picture, which does not lend itself to a pleasing composition. The best shaped blossoms on vertical stems are usually found well up in the tree, so a ladder is frequently necessary to reach them.

Another attractive member of the Magnolia family is the Star Magnolia (Fig. 63). The double, white flowers consist of a dozen or more slender petals. When radiographed, the image looks like an artist, very skilled in the use of charcoal, had drawn it.

Some flowers are pretty to look at, but in a radiograph they display very little interesting detail in the petals. The Squash blossom, on the other hand, is extremely rich in beautiful details (Fig. 85). The elaborate system of veins, the frilly edges of the petals and even the tiniest hairs are recorded in this radiograph. It causes one to wonder why such a lovely flower was created to last for only one day.

In addition to trees like the Dogwood (Fig. 35) and Magnolia (Fig. 62), with their large showy blossoms, other trees, whose wood is used commercially, also have interesting flowers. Examples of these are Birch (Fig. 8), Box Elder (Fig. 10), Hickory (Fig. 47), Maple (Fig. 64) and Oak (Fig. 67).

Some plants with insignificant looking blossoms produce seeds and associated parts that have very interesting shapes. Examples of these are the Chinese Lantern (Fig. 19), Goat's Beard (Fig. 45), Yellow Bristle Grass (Figs. 11 and 12) and Foxtail Chess (Fig. 40). A seed bearing stalk of Foxtail Chess results in a serene image which looks as though it were drawn by a very skilful Oriental artist.

Over thirty years of experimentation with this unusual art form has led to its present high degree of excellence. Floral radiographs literally provide one with a third eye with which to see and appreciate the beauty of the secret garden.

TECHNICAL CONSIDERATIONS

Floral radiographs are produced by placing the flower between the X-ray machine and the film. Either cut or potted flowers can be used with the film positioned vertically and the X-ray beam directed horizontally. Cut flowers can be supported for exposure, by enclosing the end of the stem in modeling clay or in a small tube containing water.

The sharpness of the image depends on the type of film that is used, along with geometric factors, such as size of the focal spot of the X-ray tube, the distance between the X-ray tube and the flower, and the distance from the flower to the film. The sharpest images, made with the least enlargement, are produced by placing the flower as close to the film as possible and as far from the X-ray as is practical. The time of exposure increases rapidly as this latter distance is increased. Ideally, the film should be located between two to five feet from the X-ray tube. Water or oil cooling of the anode of the X-ray tube is desirable to prevent damage to the focal spot during long exposures. Dental X-ray machines are not suitable for making floral radiographs. The best floral radiographs are produced with beryllium window X-ray tubes. Only some medical and industrial X-ray machines have this desirable feature.

Depending on the makeup of the flower, the proper tube voltage lies in a range from 20 to 30 kilovolts peak. Thick succulent petals record properly at higher voltages, while thin, fragile petals register better at lower values.

By law, dental and medical X-ray machines must have a certain amount of inherent plus added filtration present before the machine can be used with human beings. For floral radiography, only the inherent filtration of the beryllium window of the X-ray tube is employed.

X-ray films are made with a sensitive emulsion layer on one or both sides of the film base. Any X-ray film can be used in producing a floral radiograph, however, the second emulsion layer is of small benefit in this application because the major portion of the image will be recorded in the first emulsion layer. This is because the attenuation of these low energy X rays by the film base is considerable, and not much of the radiation ever reaches the second emulsion. Generally, higher speed films produce more granular images than do the slower films. Excellent floral radiographs can be made using any type of fine grain X-ray film. For floral radiography, the film can be exposed while uncovered, if the room is lighted with an appropriate safelight; otherwise, the film must be wrapped in a very thin sheet of opaque plastic.

The proper time of exposure must be determined by trial and error, since it is determined by such variables as the type of flower, the speed of the film, the distance between the X-ray tube and the film, the X-ray tube voltage and current and whether the film is to be used bare or wrapped.

PHOTOGRAPHIC CONSIDERATIONS

After an exposed X-ray film has been processed, it can be treated as any other negative to make either a contact or enlarged print. However, it may display a wider range of densities than is found on conventional photographic negatives.

The use of 5″×7″ X-ray film limits the size of a flower that can be recorded. This size of film also requires a 5″×7″ enlarging camera which is rather expensive and not commonly found in the average photographer's darkroom. Larger flowers can be recorded on larger films, which then can be photographically copied onto a smaller format film. This in turn can be used with enlarging cameras of a more common or popular size.

An understanding of photographic processes is recommended in order to produce the best possible floral radiographs. Contact prints or enlargements made from radiographs display dark images with light backgrounds. The production of light images with dark backgrounds, similar to the radiographic image, requires one additional step. If the radiograph is considered to be a negative, a contact positive must be made on a continuous tone film, which is then used to produce the desired dark image picture.

Radiographs frequently display a much wider range of photographic densities than can be reproduced on photographic paper. Regardless of the grade of paper that is used, it is difficult to portray details in both the highlighted and darker areas of the picture at the same time. Various techniques are available to help remedy this problem. A contrast-reducing technique, known as "flashing" adds just enough extra density to darken the highlights without noticeably affecting the other details. The correct duration of the "flash" is determined by exposing a test piece of photographic paper to an increasing series of white light exposures. Upon development, the longest exposure that produced no visible effect upon the paper is the proper exposure time for "flashing." After the paper has been "flashed," it is exposed and processed in the usual manner to produce contact prints or enlargements.

Another contrast-reducing technique, which adds density to the highlight details and not the shadows, involves nothing more exotic than a tray of fresh water. First, expose the paper normally; then place it in the developer bath. When the image begins to appear, quickly transfer the print to a tray of fresh water. This step, which requires no agitation, removes developer solution from the surface of the print. The developer, absorbed by the emulsion, is quickly used up in the dark areas of the image, and further development ceases. In the highlight areas of the image, the absorbed developer is exhausted more slowly and development of details in the area continues. After about one minute, return the print to the developer, agitate for a few seconds, then transfer back to the water bath. Alternate between the developer and the water until development is complete.

The following is a technique designed to portray the details of the darkest areas that would otherwise be lost in a print. It is a variation of the "Sabattier effect" and it works best with #4 or #5 grade enlarging paper. Replace the easel of the enlarging camera with an overturned processing tray with a smooth flat bottom. With a permanent black ink felt-tip pen draw the outline of a sheet of enlarging paper on the bottom of the tray. Place a spare sheet of paper within this rectangle, then focus and compose the picture on it with the enlarging camera's lens wide open. Next, stop down the lens to f22, or as small as possible. Under safelight conditions, place an unexposed sheet of enlarging paper in the developer bath for one minute; then lift it out and hold it vertically for thirty seconds while the developer drains off the paper. While touching only the back surface of the enlarging paper, carefully place the damp paper within the back outlined rectangle on the overturned tray. DO NOT TOUCH THE EMULSION SURFACE. Turn on the enlarger for a few seconds. The proper number of seconds is quite exacting and must be determined by trial and error. Wait one minute while the images of details in the darkest shadows appear. During this waiting period, open the lens one stop or more and then give a second exosure of sufficient length that will yield satisfactory highlight details. Immediately place the paper in the developer bath and then follow normal processing steps. Beautiful examples of this technique are shown in Figures 27, 35, 45, 52, 62 and 94.

Other methods for modifying the image that appears on the print would include shading (dodging), burning in, the use of Polycontrast paper with various filters for exposing different areas on the paper, the application of concentrated developer with a brush to certain places on the print to accentuate details in isolated areas, diluting the developer, the use of soft-acting and solarizing developers.

Solarization of a print occurs while it is in the solarizing developer solution. After the image starts to appear on the paper, an overhead white light is turned on briefly, and then the development is allowed to continue to completion. A solarized picture generally has a dark background with a lighter image. It is neither a negative nor a positive image, but is somewhere in between the two. Where there is an abrupt change in contrast in the radiograph, such as is caused by a stem, a thin white line appears in the solarized print. Examples of both normal and solarized images of the same blossom are seen in Figures 11 and 12, 20 and 21, 23 and 24, 25 and 26, 48 and 49, 88 and 89 and lastly 95 and 96.

An example of a stereo pair of floral images of a Hyacinth blossom is shown in Figure 51. After the first of this pair was made, the flower was rotated 3 degrees about its vertical axis, and then the second image was recorded. The rotation of the flower was necessary so the two images would correspond to what your left and right eyes would see, if somehow magically, you were gifted with X-ray vision. It is a well known fact, that since one's eyes are spaced approximately 2⅝ inches apart, that each eye sees objects from a slightly different angle. When focusing on a nearby object, the lines ofsight from the eyes converge at about a 3 degree angle.

To view a pair of stereographs in three dimensions, usually requires the observer to use a stereoscope (an optical viewing device with two lenses). However, it is possible to learn to look at the left-hand picture of the stereo pair with the left eye while the right eye is focused on the right-hand picture. This is the "free vision" method for viewing stereographs. While learning this method, some persons have found it helpful to hold a piece of cardboard up to their nose to prevent the right eye from seeing the left-hand picture, and the left-hand eye from seeing the right-hand image. It is a skill that requires much practice to master, but once learned, is very satisfying.

LIST OF FLOWERS

Figure 1 Amaryllis <u>Hippeastrum</u> <u>Puniceum</u>
Figure 2 Apple Blossoms <u>Malus</u> <u>pumila</u>
Figure 3 Ash Tree, Mountain <u>Sorbus</u> <u>aucuparia</u>
Figure 4 Aster <u>Amelius</u> <u>annuus</u>
Figure 5 Azalea <u>Rhododendron</u> species
Figure 6 Begonia, Tuberous Rooted <u>Begonia</u> Tuberhybrida Group
Figure 7 Bells of Ireland <u>Moluccella</u> <u>laevis</u>
Figure 8 Birch Tree <u>Betula</u> species
Figure 9 Bleeding Heart <u>Dicentra</u> <u>spectabilis</u>
Figure 10 Box Elder Tree <u>Acer</u> <u>negundo</u>
Figure 11 Bristlegrass, Yellow <u>Setaria</u> <u>lutescens</u>
Figure 12 Bristlegrass, Yellow <u>Setaria</u> <u>lutescens</u> (Solarized)
Figure 13 Cactus, Thanksgiving <u>Schlumbergera</u> <u>truncata</u>
Figure 14 Calla Lily <u>Zantedeschia</u> <u>aethiopica</u>
Figure 15 Campanula, Cup and Saucer <u>Campanula</u> <u>medium</u> 'Calycanthema'
Figure 16 Cherry, Kwanzan <u>Prunus</u> <u>serrulata</u> 'Kwanzan'
Figure 17 Cherry, Weeping <u>Prunus</u> <u>serrulata</u> 'Pendula'
Figure 18 Chicory <u>Cichorium</u> <u>intybus</u>
Figure 19 Chinese Lanterns <u>Physalis</u> <u>alkekengi</u>
Figure 20 Chrysanthemum <u>Chrysanthemum</u> (Spoon Type)
Figure 21 Chrysanthemum <u>Chrysanthemum</u> (Spoon Type) (Solarized)
Figure 22 Clematis <u>Clematis</u> 'Jackmani'
Figure 23 Crocus, Saffron <u>Crocus</u> <u>sativus</u>
Figure 24 Crocus, Saffron <u>Crocus</u> <u>sativus</u> (Solarized)
Figure 25 Columbine with bud <u>Aquilegia</u> 'McKana Hybrid'
Figure 26 Columbine with bud <u>Aquilegia</u> 'McKana Hybrid' (Solarized)
Figure 27 Cosmos <u>Cosmos</u> <u>sulphureus</u>
Figure 28 Cyclamen, Frilly <u>Cyclamen</u> <u>persicum</u> (Frilly cultivar)
Figure 29 Cyclamen, Florist's <u>Cyclamen</u> <u>persicum</u>
Figure 30 Daffodil <u>Narcissus</u> 'King Alfred'
Figure 31 Daffodil, Peruvian <u>Hymenocallis</u> <u>narcissiflora</u>
Figure 32 Dahlia, Cactus <u>Dahlia</u> cultivar
Figure 33 Daisy, Ox-Eye <u>Chrysanthemum</u> <u>leucanthemum</u>
Figure 34 Daylily <u>Hemerocallis</u> cultivar
Figure 35 Dogwood, Flowering <u>Cornus</u> <u>florida</u>
Figure 36 Elderberry, American <u>Sambucus</u> <u>canadensis</u>
Figure 37 Eucalyptus, Silver-dollar <u>Eucalyptus</u> <u>polyanthemos</u>
Figure 38 Forsythia <u>Forsythia</u> <u>x intermedia</u>
Figure 39 Foxglove <u>Digitalis</u> <u>purpurea</u>

Figure 1 Amaryllis *Hippeastrum puniceum*

Figure 2
Apple Blossoms
Malus pumila

Figure 3
Ash Tree, Mountain
Sorbus *aucuparia*

Figure 4 Aster
Amelius annuus

Figure 5   Azalea
Rhododendron species

Figure 6
Begonia, Tuberous Rooted
Begonia Tuberhybrida Group

Figure 7
Bells of Ireland <u>*Moluccella*</u> <u>*laevis*</u>

Figure 8   Birch Tree <u>Betula</u> species

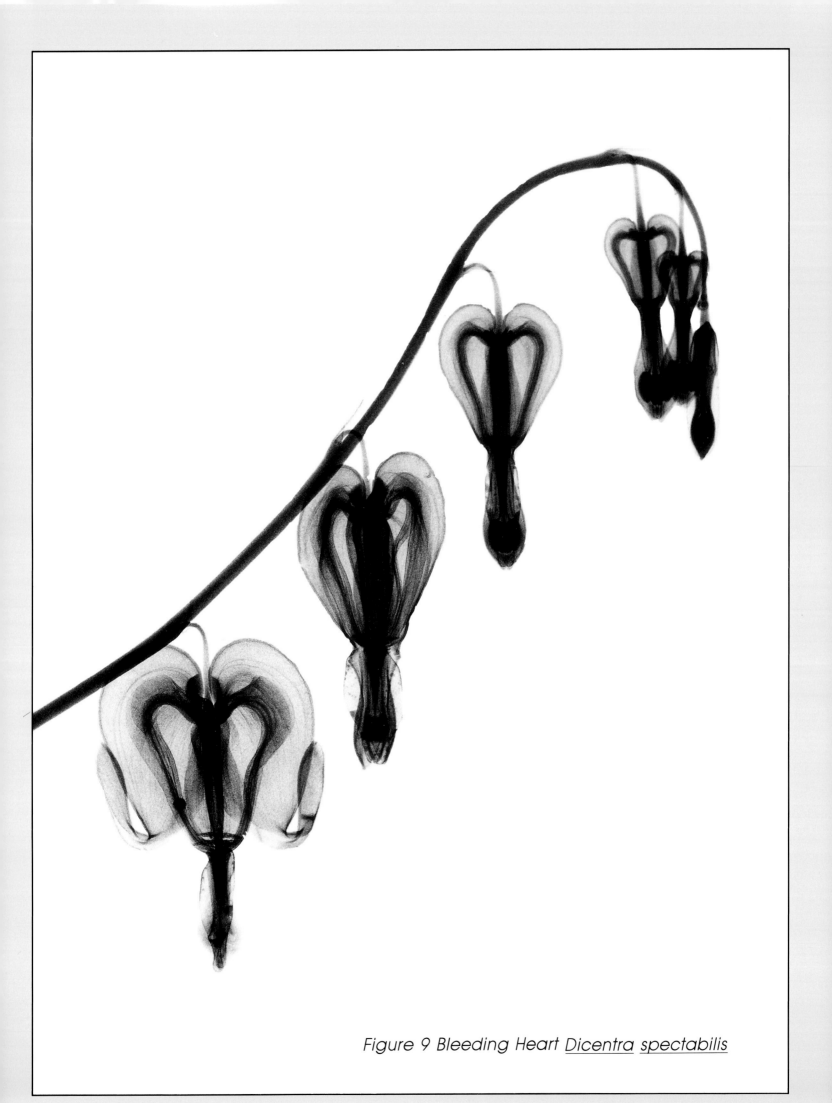

Figure 9 Bleeding Heart <u>Dicentra</u> <u>spectabilis</u>

Figure 10
Box Elder Tree <u>Acer</u> <u>negundo</u>

Figure 11   Bristlegrass, Yellow
<u>*Setaria*</u> <u>*lutescens*</u>

Figure 12 Bristlegrass,
Yellow *Setaria* *lutescens*
(Solarized)

Figure 13
Cactus, Thanksgiving
Schlumbergera *truncata*

Figure 14
Calla Lily <u>Zantedeschia</u> <u>aethiopica</u>

Figure 15 Campanula, Cup and Saucer
<u>*Campanula*</u> <u>*medium*</u> *'Calycanthema'*

Figure 16   Cherry, Kwanzan <u>Prunus</u> <u>serrulata</u> 'Kwanzan'

Figure 17
Cherry, Weeping <u>Prunus</u> <u>serrulata</u> 'Pendula'

Figure 18
Chicory <u>*Cichorium*</u> <u>*intybus*</u>

Figure 19
Chinese Lanterns <u>Physalis</u> <u>alkekengi</u>

Figure 20
Chrysanthemum
<u>*Chrysanthemum*</u>
(Spoon Type)

Figure 21
Chrysanthemum
Chrysanthemum
(Spoon Type) (Solarized)

Figure 22   Clematis <u>Clematis</u> 'Jackmani'

Figure 23
Crocus, Saffron <u>Crocus</u> <u>sativus</u>

Figure 24   Crocus, Saffron
Crocus sativus (Solarized)

Figure 25   Columbine with bud
Aquilegia 'McKana Hybrid'

Figure 26 Columbine with bud
<u>*Aquilegia*</u> *'McKana Hybrid' (Solarized)*

Figure 27   Cosmos
Cosmos sulphureus

*Figure 28   Cyclamen,
Frilly Cyclamen persicum
(Frilly cultivar)*

Figure 29   Cyclamen,
Florist's <u>Cyclamen</u> <u>persicum</u>

Figure 30
Daffodil <u>Narcissus</u> 'King Alfred'

Figure 31 Daffodil,
Peruvian _Hymenocallis_ _narcissiflora_

Figure 32
Dahlia, Cactus <u>Dahlia</u> cultivar

Figure 33 Daisy, Ox-Eye <u>Chrysanthemum</u> <u>leucanthemum</u>

Figure 34   Daylily *Hemerocallis* cultivar

Figure 35   Dogwood,
Flowering *Cornus* *florida*

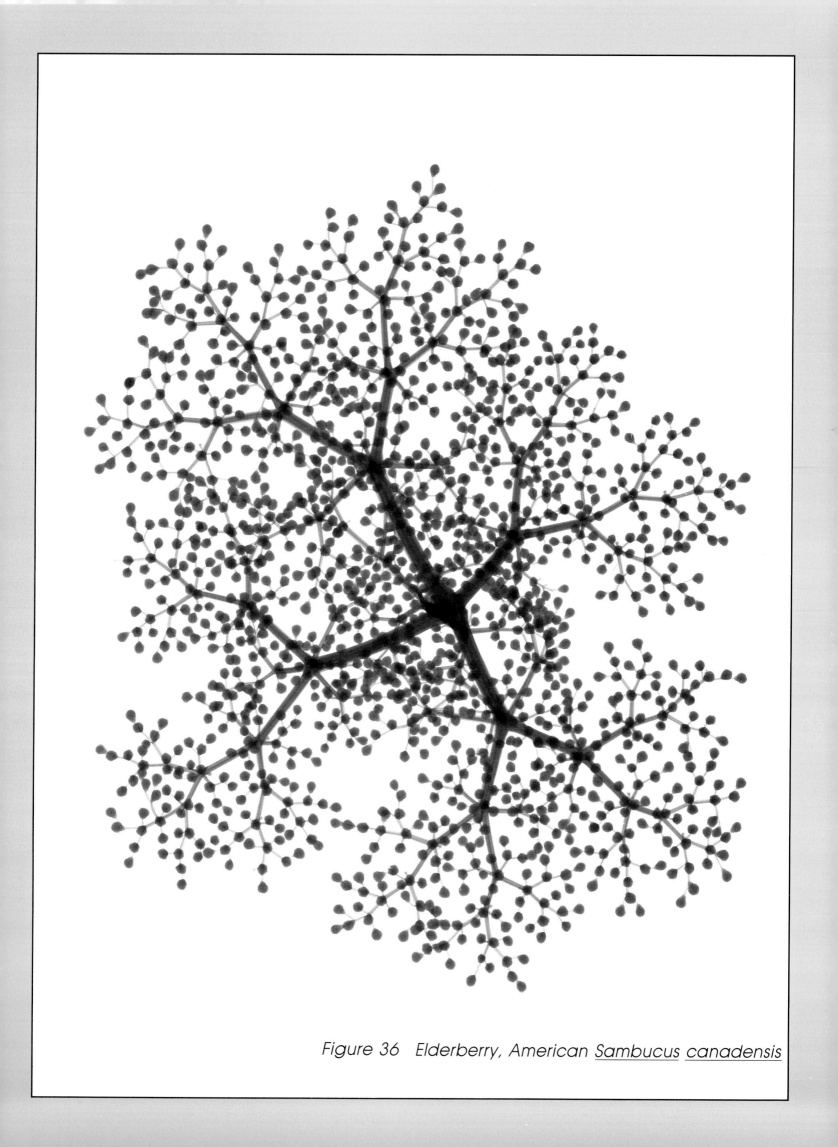

Figure 36   Elderberry, American Sambucus canadensis

Figure 37
Eucalyptus, Silver-dollar
Eucalyptus polyanthemos

Figure 38   Forsythia _Forsythia_ x _intermedia_

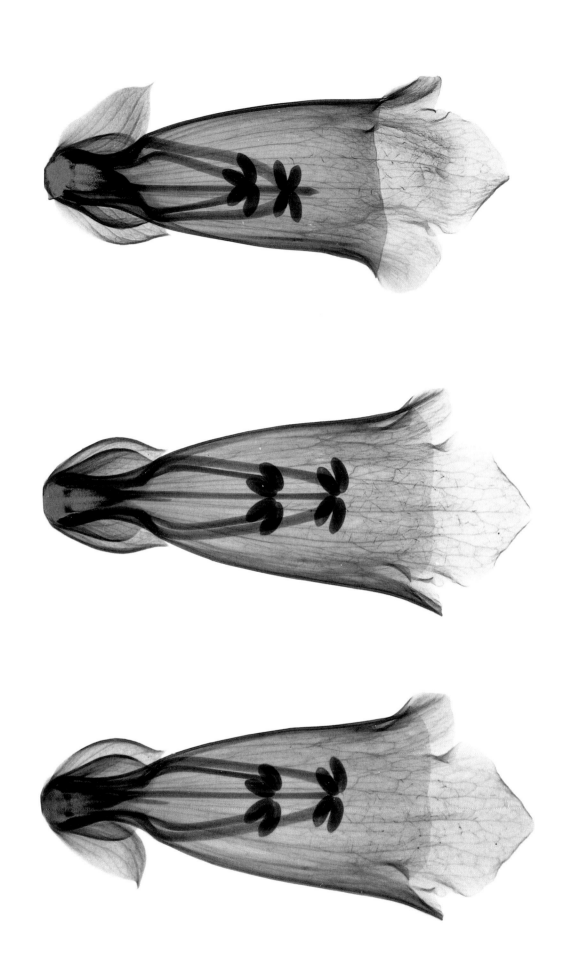

Figure 39 Foxglove Digitalis purpurea

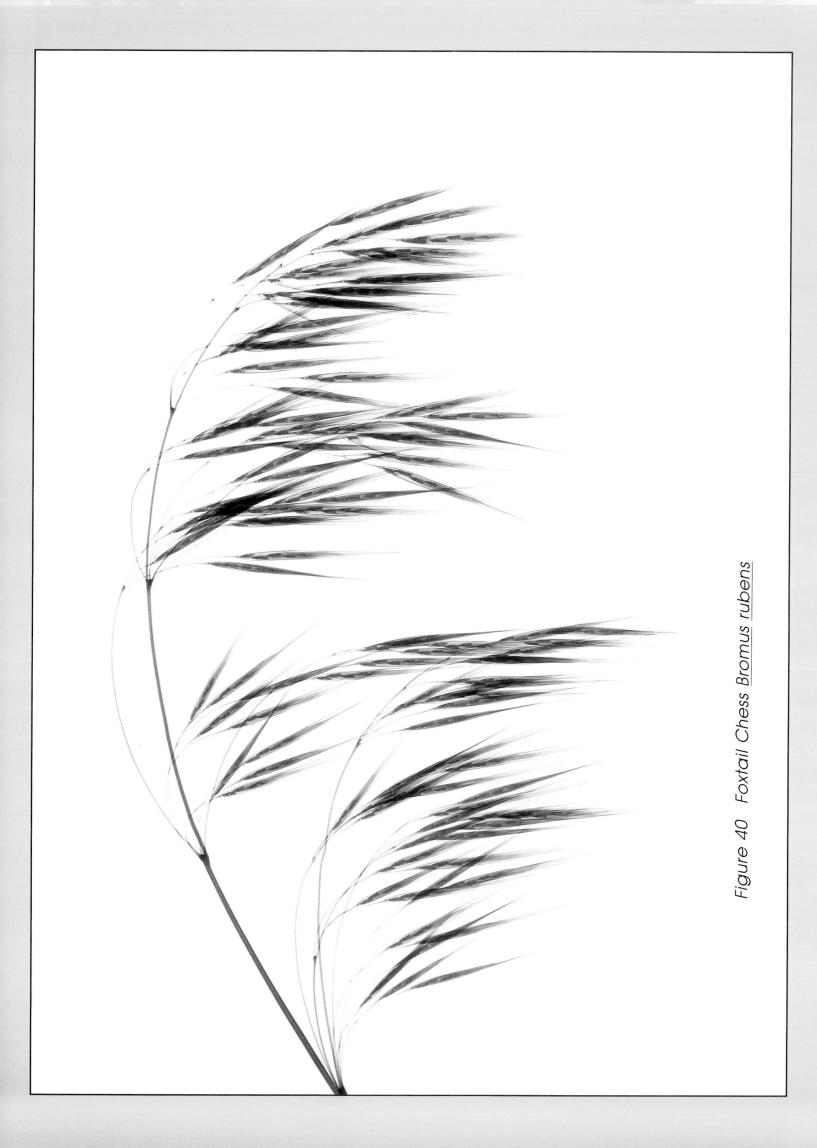

Figure 40 Foxtail Chess *Bromus rubens*

Figure 41   Freesia <u>Freesia</u> <u>x hybrida</u>

Figure 42   Fuchsia *Fuchsia* *arboresens*

Figure 43   Gladiolus <u>Gladiolus</u> <u>x hortulanus</u>

Figure 44
Gloxinia with bud <u>*Sinningia*</u> <u>*speciosa*</u>

Figure 45
Goat's Beard *Tragopogon pratensis*

Figure 46   Hibiscus Hibiscus rosa-sinensis

Figure 47   Hickory, Shagbark <u>Carya</u> <u>ovata</u>

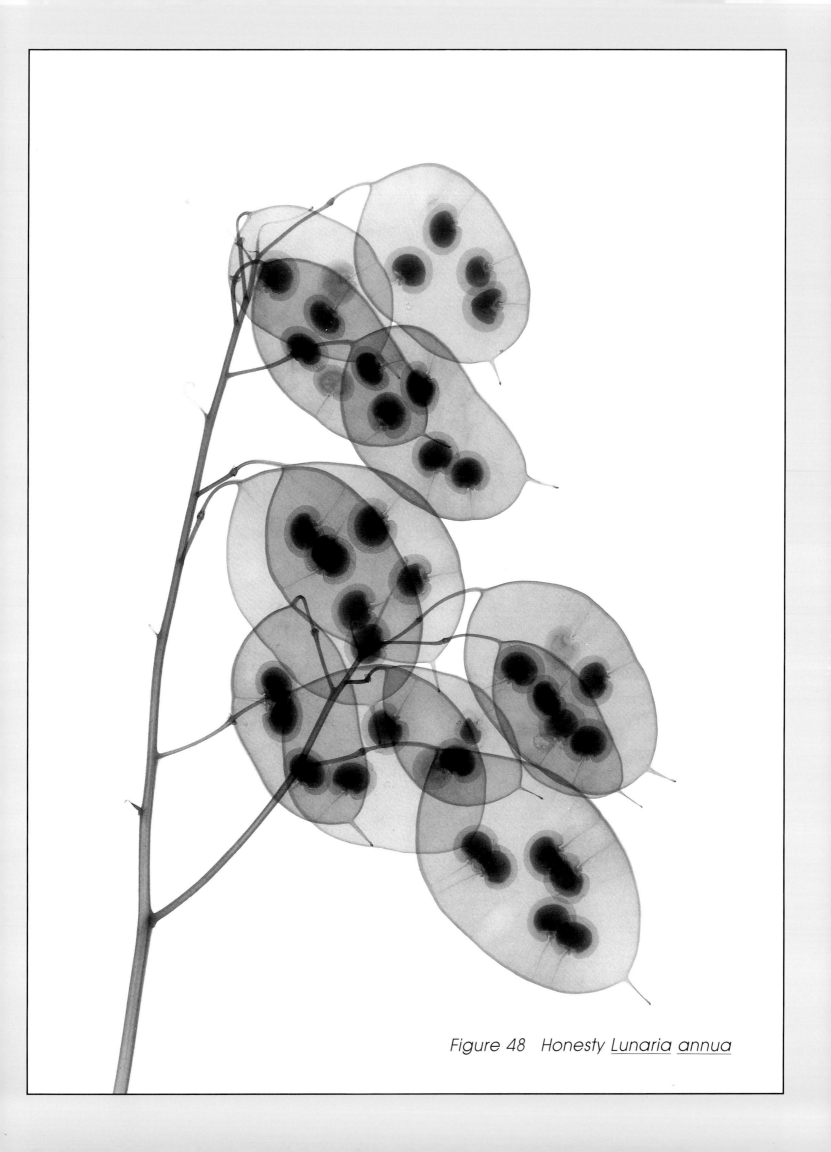

Figure 48   Honesty <u>Lunaria</u> <u>annua</u>

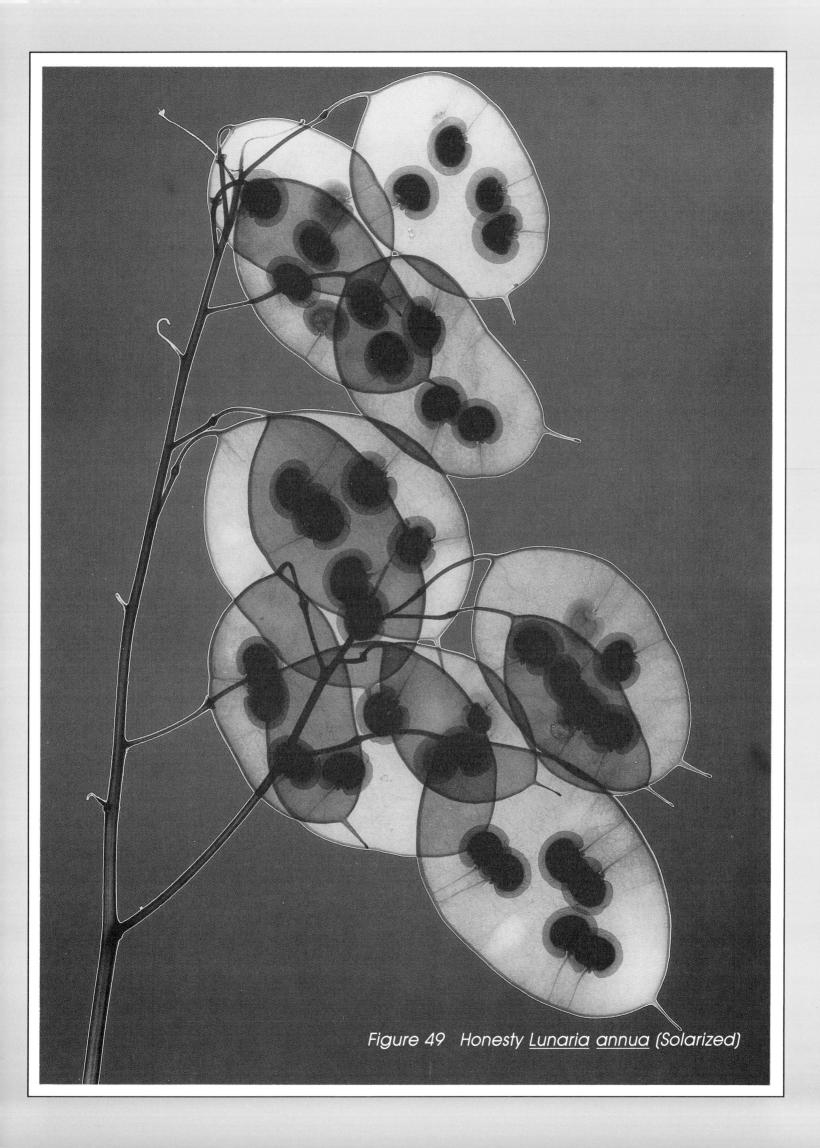

Figure 49   Honesty Lunaria annua (Solarized)

Figure 50
Hyacinth <u>*Hyacinthus*</u> <u>*orientalis*</u>

Figure 51 Hyacinth *Hyacinthus orientalis* (Stereo pair)

Figure 52   Iris, German <u>Iris</u> *cultivar*

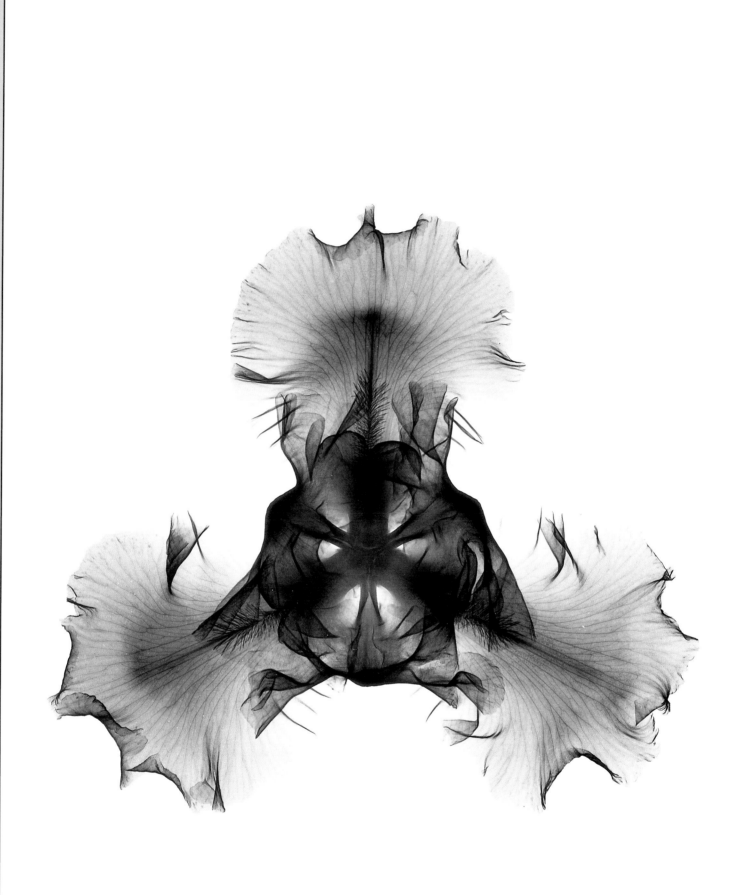

Figure 53
Iris, German <u>Iris</u> cultivar Top view

Figure 54   Iris, Spanish <u>Iris</u> <u>xiphium</u>

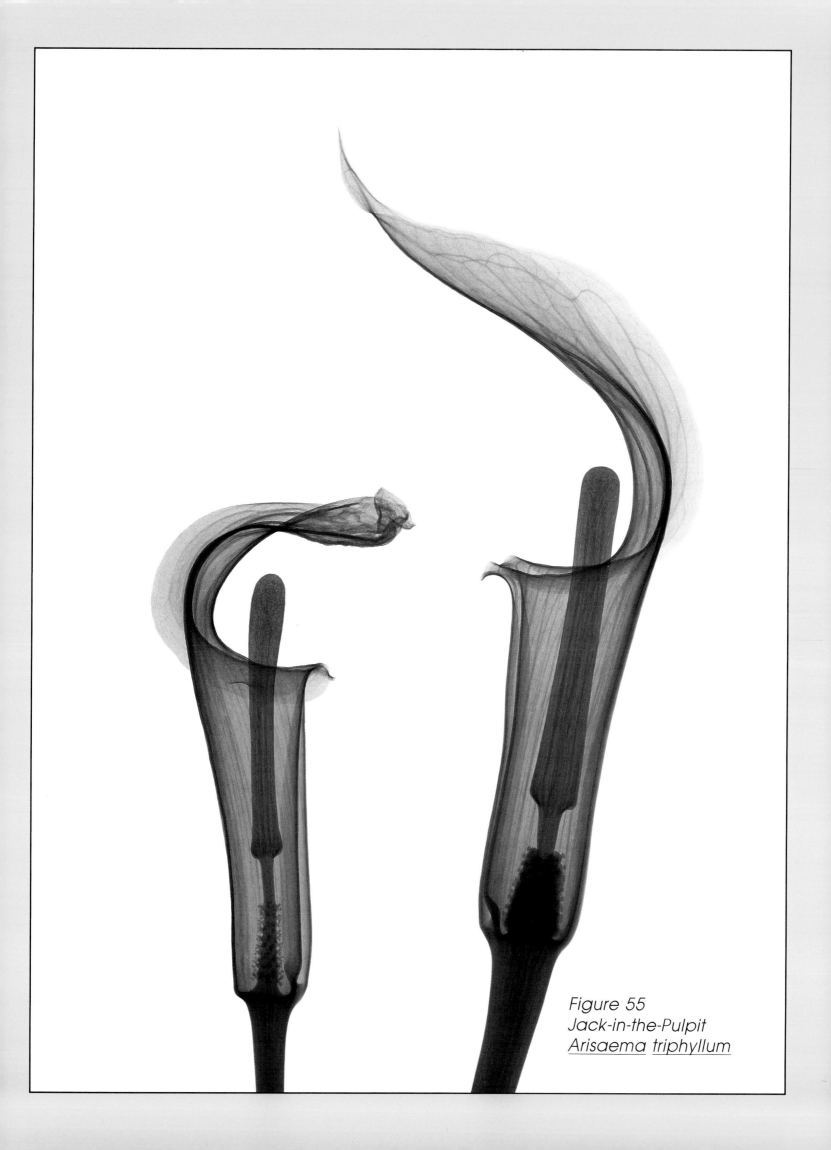

Figure 55
Jack-in-the-Pulpit
Arisaema triphyllum

Figure 56 Lady Slipper
Cypripedium candidum

Figure 57 Larkspur <u>Delphinium</u> cultivar

Figure 58 Lily, Aztec <u>Sprekalia</u> <u>formosissima</u>

Figure 59   Lily <u>Lilium</u> 'Casablanca'

Figure 60
Lipstick Plant <u>*Aeschynanthus*</u> <u>*pulcher*</u>

Figure 61   Lisianthus with bud
Eustoma grandiflorum

Figure 62   Magnolia,
Saucer <u>Magnolia</u> <u>x soulangiana</u>

Figure 63   Magnolia, Star <u>Magnolia</u> <u>stellata</u>

Figure 64   Maple Tree Acer species

Figure 65   Mock Orange
Philadelphus coronarius

Figure 66   Monkshood <u>Aconitum</u> <u>napellus</u>

Figure 67   Oak, Pin Quercus palustris

Figure 68   Oats, Wild
Chasmanthium latifolium

Figure 69   Orchid <u>Paphiopedilum</u> cultivar

Figure 70   Orchid *Angraecum species*

Figure 71   Passion Flower <u>Passiflora</u> <u>caerulea</u>

Figure 72   Peony <u>Paeonia</u> <u>lactiflora</u> cultivar

Figure 73   Peruvian Lily
Alstroemeria aurantiacus

Figure 74   Pincushion Flower
Leucospermum nutans

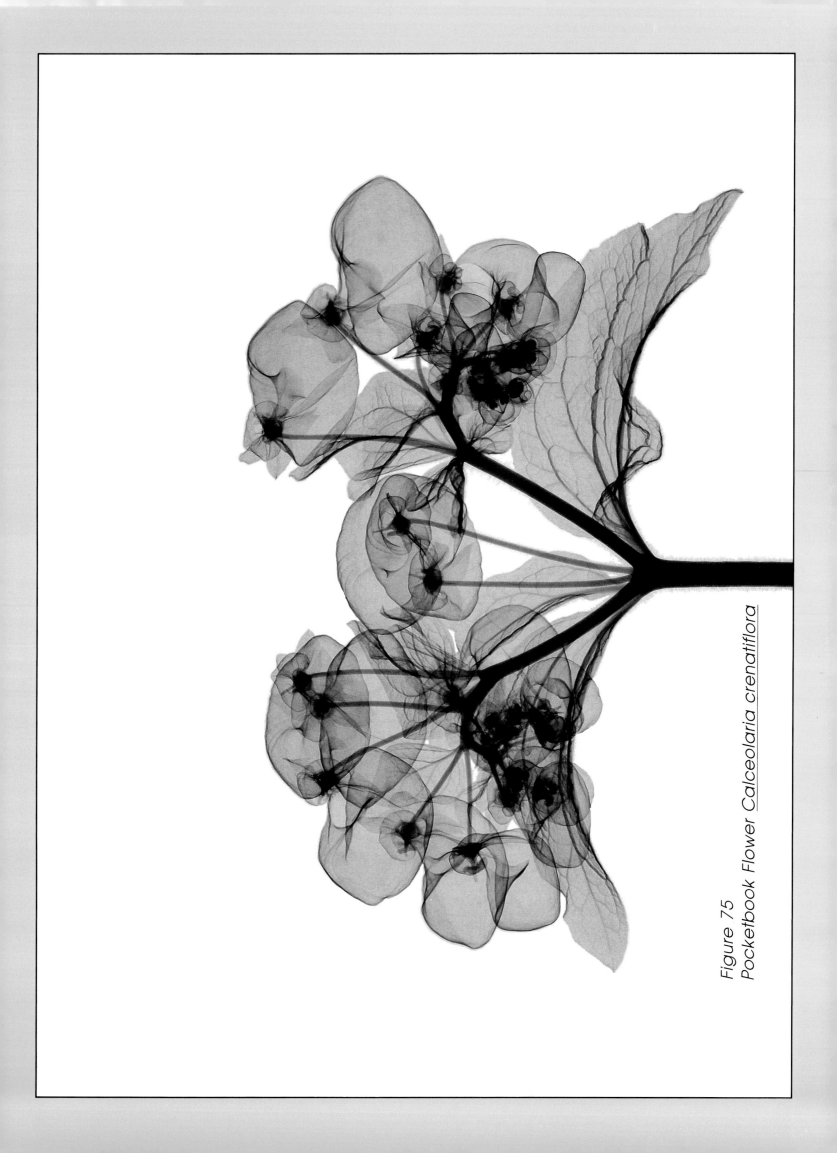

Figure 75
Pocketbook Flower Calceolaria crenatiflora

Figure 76 Poppy, Oriental <u>Papaver</u> <u>orientale</u>

Figure 77
Powderpuff Plant
Calliandra haematocephala

Figure 78 Pussy Willow _Salix_ _discolor_

*Figure 79 Queen Anne's Lace,
Wild Carrot <u>Daucus</u> <u>carota</u>*

Figure 80   Rose,
Hybrid Tea <u>Rosa</u> 'Tropicana'

Figure 81   Rose, Top View <u>Rosa</u> cultivar

Figure 82 Rose of Sharon
Hibiscus syriacus

Figure 83
Skunk Cabbage with Spider
Symplocarpus foetidus

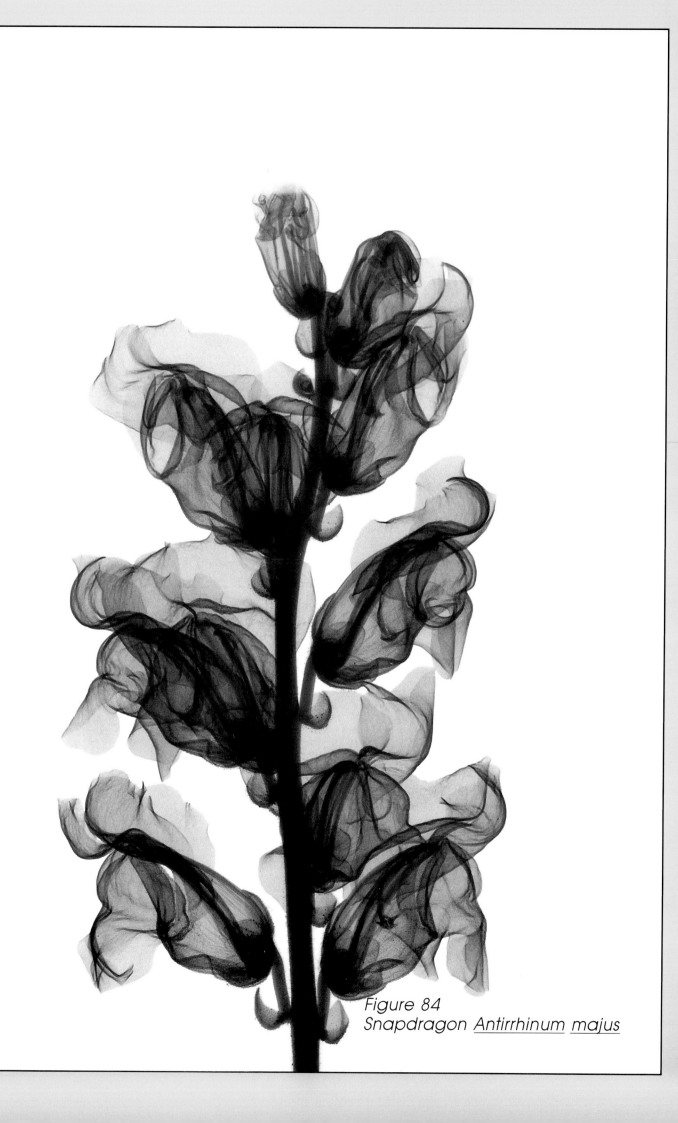

Figure 84
Snapdragon <u>Antirrhinum</u> <u>majus</u>

Figure 85   Squash <u>Cucurbita</u> <u>pepo</u>

*Figure 86 Sunflower,
Common <u>Helianthus</u> <u>annuus</u>*

Figure 87   Sweet Peas Lathyrus odoratus

Figure 88
Thistle <u>Cirsium</u> <u>arvense</u>

Figure 89   Thistle
<u>*Cirsium*</u> <u>*arvense*</u> *(Solarized)*

Figure 90
Tiger Flower <u>*Tigridia*</u> <u>*pavonia*</u>

Figure 91   Tobacco,
Sweet <u>Nicotiana</u> <u>x sanderae</u>

Figure 92   Tulip Tulipa cultivar

Figure 93   Tulip with bud <u>Tulipa</u> cultivar

Figure 94   Tulip top view <u>Tulipa</u> cultivar

Figure 95   Viburnum
Viburnum plicatum 'Mariesii'

Figure 96 Viburnum
Viburnum plicatum 'Mariesii' (Solarized)

Figure 97   Water Lily *Nymphaea* cultivar

Figure 98 Willow Tree _Salix babylonica_

Figure 99   Yucca <u>Yucca</u> species

Figure 100 Zinnia <u>Zinnia</u> <u>elegans</u>

About the Author

Albert G. Richards was born in Chicago in 1917. His training in photography began at an early age, because his father was a professional photographer. Formal training at the University of Michigan led to degrees in Chemical Engineering and Physics. In 1940 he joined the School of Dentistry Staff as an Instructor and focused his interest on x-ray photography and its application to dentistry by teaching himself dental radiography. By 1959 he was made Professor and in 1974 was named the Marcus L. Ward Professor of Dentistry, the first distinguished professorship at the Dental School. His teaching career at Michigan spanned more than four decades.

A creative, inventive researcher and outstanding teacher, Professor Richards is known as one of the world's foremost authorities in the field of dental radiography. He has earned many honors for his teaching and research, including establishment by the School of the Albert G. Richards Award for Excellence in Radiography, which is given annually to a student.

Among his many accomplishments are the invention of the recessed cone dental x-ray head (now found in many dental offices), being the first to use the electron microscope to see the microstructure of human teeth, and inventing the liquid mold technique for showing, with x-rays, the topography of surfaces. This technique has been applied in such diverse fields as fingerprinting and identification, botany, paleobotany, art and archeology. Other products of his inventive mind are dynamic tomography, a radiographic procedure that allows scientists to examine successively, an infinite number of thin layers of an object, and devising the Buccal Object Rule, a radiographic procedure for determining the relative location of objects hidden in the oral region. He also holds six patents on his inventions, is the author of more than 100 publications and is a member of several professional organizations.

He and his wife raised their five daughters in a beautiful house he built with his own hands. In retirement, he is kept busy pursuing his avocation — the radiographing of flowers. Examples of his unusual and beautiful art have appeared in prominent magazines around the world, in museums, in encyclopedias and on calendars.